Incredible Insects

Zoe Barnes

SCHOLASTIC INC.

NEW YORK • TORONTO • LONDON • AUCKLAND • SYDNEY
MEXICO CITY • NEW DELHI • HONG KONG • BUENOS AIRES

ISBN-13: 978-0-545-06083-7 / ISBN-10: 0-545-06083-4

Photo Credits:

Cover © Darrell Gulin/Getty Images; title page: © Tim Fitzharris/Minden Pictures; contents page, from top: © Heinrich van den Berg/Getty Images, © Jane Burton/Nature Picture Library, © Gail Shumway/Getty Images; © Mark Moffett/Minden Pictures; page 4: © Heinrich van den Berg/Getty Images; page 5: © Kim Taylor/Nature Picture Library; page 5, inset: © Kim Taylor/Nature Picture Library; page 6: © Stephen Dalton/Minden Pictures; page 6, inset: © Jef Meul/Getty Images; page 7: all © Kim Taylor/NPL/Minden Pictures; page 8: © Jane Burton/Nature Picture Library; page 9, left: © Stephen Dalton/OSF/Animals Animals; page 9, right: © Piotr Naskrecki/Minden Pictures; page 10: © Karen Moskowitz/Getty Images; page 11: © Ingo Arndt/Minden Pictures: page 12: © Gail Shumway/Getty Images; page 13: © David M. Dennis/Animals Animals; page 13, inset: © Mark Moffett/Minden Pictures; page 14: © Mitsuhiko Imarmori/Minden Pictures; page 14, inset: © William Osborn/Minden Pictures; page 15: © Stephen Dalton/Minden Pictures; back cover: © Morley Read/Nature Picture Library.

Photo research by Dwayne Howard
Design by Holly Grundon

12 11 10 9 8 11 12 13 14/0

Printed in the U.S.A. 40
First printing, January 2009

Contents

Chapter 1

Meet the Insects

shorthorn grasshopper

Insects may be tiny. But take a close look. You will see that they are incredible!

Insect Parts

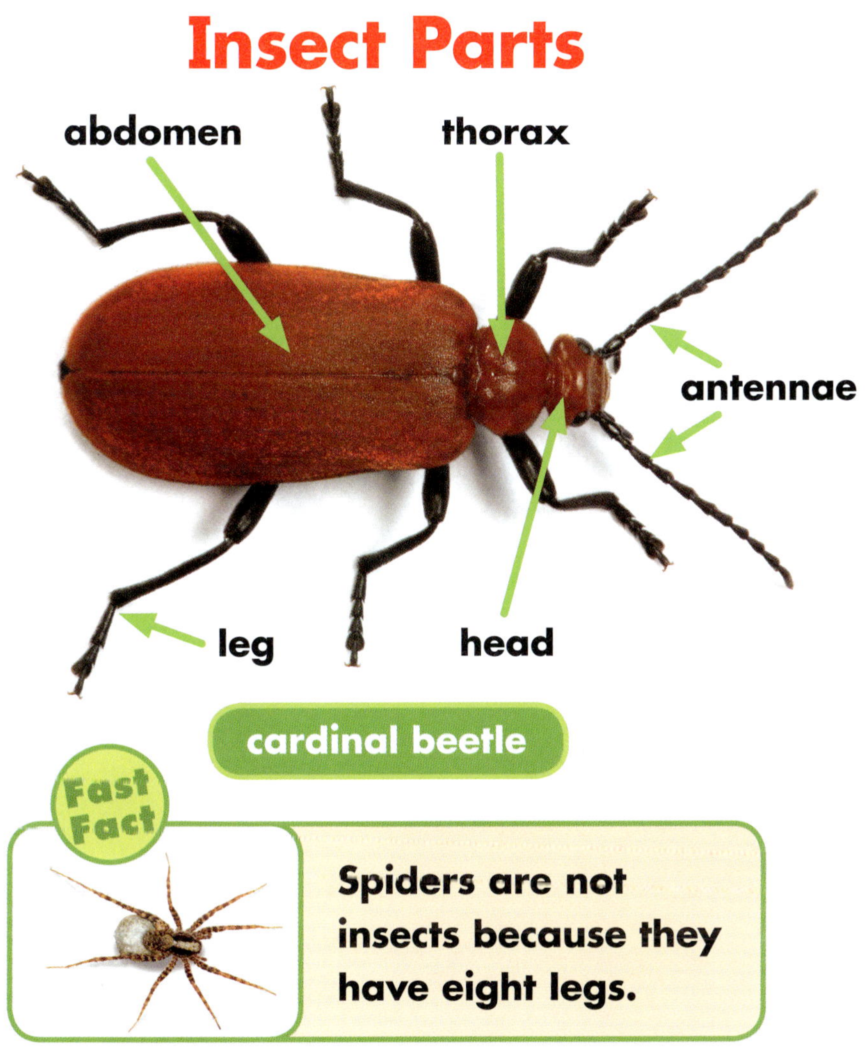

cardinal beetle

Fast Fact

Spiders are not insects because they have eight legs.

What makes an insect an insect? All insects have three body parts: head, thorax, and abdomen. They also have six legs and two **antennae**.

All insects have a hard covering called an **exoskeleton**. This protects their soft insides.

The World's Animals

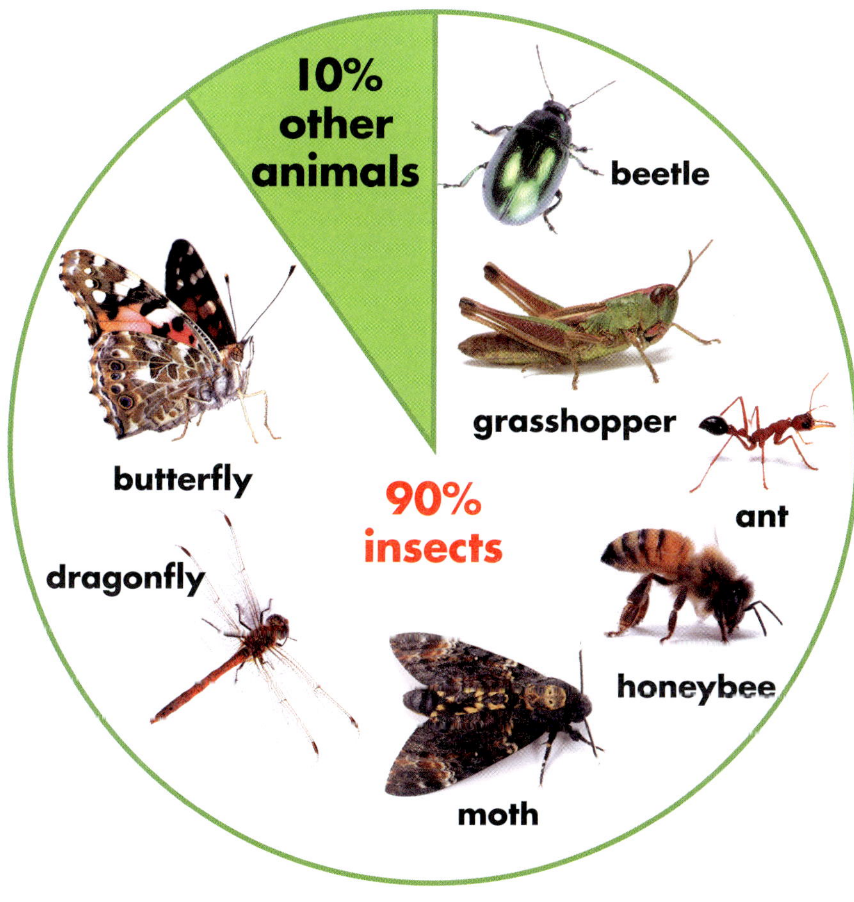

Insects are the most common kind of creature on earth. Ninety percent of the world's animals are insects. Let's learn all about them!

Chapter 2

Insect Skills

diving beetle

Insects are very **adaptable**. They live in hot places and cold places. They live in trees and on the ground. Some even live in the water. Splash!

Many insects taste with their feet.

horsefly

katydid

Insects have **keen** senses that are different from other animals. The eyes of a horsefly have thousands of tiny **lenses**. The ears of a katydid are on its legs.

honeybee hive

Many insects are **social** animals. They live and work together in large groups called **colonies**. One hive can have 80,000 bees!

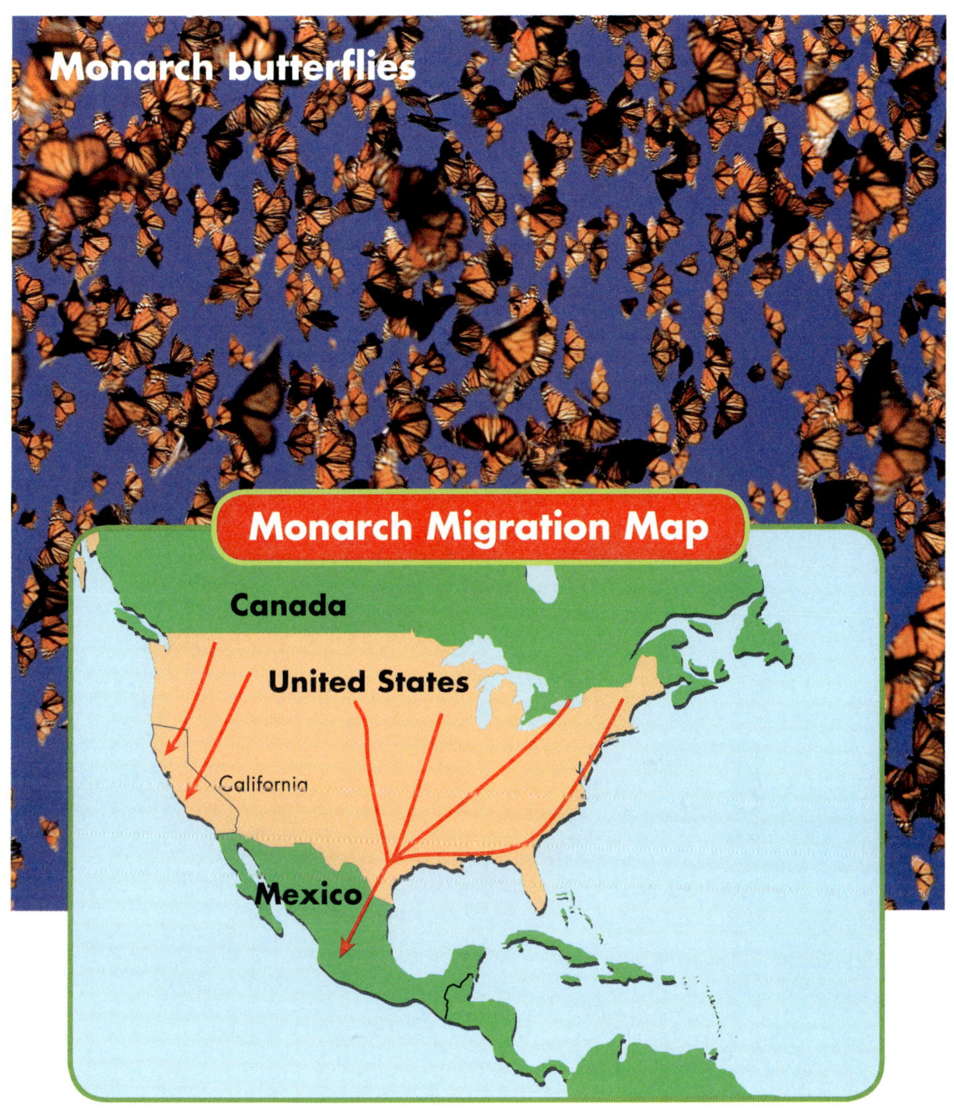

There are even insects that migrate. Monarch butterflies travel to warmer places in the fall. They return to cooler places in the spring.

Chapter 3

Amazing Insects

green birdwing butterfly

Butterflies are beautiful! And some are very big. This one has a wingspan of nearly half a foot.

Ants are super strong! They can **cart** things that are 50 times their own weight. That would be like you carrying a car!

This is a termite queen.

This is a termite worker.

Fast Fact

Termites can build homes that are as tall as houses!

Termites can live a long, long time. Some termite queens live for 50 years!

grasshoppers

Fast Fact

There are more than one million different kinds of insects.

Grasshoppers are great jumpers. They can leap 20 times the length of their own bodies. Hey, come back here!

Glossary

adaptable (uh-**dapt**-a-buhl): good at adjusting to different conditions

antennae (an-**ten**-ee): feelers on the head of an insect

cart (**kart**): to carry

colony (**kol**-uh-nee): a large group of insects that live together

exoskeleton (eks-oh-**skel**-uht-uhn): hard outer shell or covering

keen (**keen**): sharp or well-developed

lens (**lenz**): the clear part of the eye that focuses light

social (**soh**-shuhl): enjoying the company of others

Comprehension Questions

1. Can you explain what makes an insect an insect?
2. Can you name five kinds of insects?
3. Which insect in this book is your very favorite? Tell why.